Hey you! Read this!

This is NOT a Microsoft
product.

This is a spoof.

This is not a software
product at all.

And it is definitely NOT
Windows 95.

If you want a real, serious
book about Windows 95,
this isn't it!

Hysteria Publications
P.O. Box 8581
Bridgeport, CT 06605
(203) 333-9399

ISBN 1-887166-04-1   Printed in the U.S.A.

Murkysoft™
WindBlows95™

A Useless Guide

The Usual Disclaimer

Murkysoft makes no claim that this software works, is compatible with anything, or even exists. If you use this software — that is, if it in fact does exist — it may very well destroy all data in your system and possibly all data in the world. If you don't use this software, we still make no claim that someone else who is using it won't access your computer via modem, network, or electrical outlet, and destroy all data in your system and in the world.

Murkysoft is not responsible for any bad thing that ever happens, real or imagined. Murkysoft is not a drooling one-eyed mega-monster bent on world domination even if it means stealing other people's ideas and using technological monopolistic tactics to force everyone to buy from us, and we resent our having even suggested that.

And one more thing. This Useless Guide is truly useless, full of half-truths, lies, and errors. It is a total waste of your time, and if you try to copy anything from it without our permission you will be sued to within an inch of your bank account. Have a nice day. And enjoy using WindBlows95!

Table of Contents

Foreword by Bill Geeks   **9**

Notations and Conventions   **11**

Welcome!   **13**

What is WindBlows95?   13
What is the Messtop Metaphor?   13

$ystem Requirements   **15**

Compatibility (i.e. "Crashing")   17
Making WindBlows95 Work Like
WindBlows3.1   18
Running WindBlows95 on a 286 or Older
Computer   18

Features   **19**

Hyperactive icons   19
Longer File Names   20
Getting to DOOS   20
How DOOS Handles Long File Names   20
Sta...sta...stability   21
The Short Circuit Bar   22
Exhumer   23

Getting Started 25

Getting Started 25
Bailing Out 33

The Basics 35

Printing to Toast 35
Hot Tips 36
Wallpaper 37
    Wallpapering a Room 37
Task Lizards 39
Navigating In the Carpal Tunnel 40

Murkysoft Orifice 42

Murkysoft Sentence 42
Murkysoft SheetLoad of Numbers 43
Murkysoft Excess 43
Other Bundled Stuff 43
    Practically Error-Free Calculator 43
    Scheduler, with Dynamic Slippage Feature 44

Installing New Hardware 45

Plug and Play 45
Pub and Pay 46

Using Networks 47

Multimedia **49**

Olfactory card 49

Thermal card 49

"Ultra" Sound Card 50

Other Special Drivers 51

Virtual Device Drivers 51

Plotter Tattoo Driver 51

Aerodynamic Fan Driver 52

Controlling the Weather 52

Bill's World **53**

Internet Voyeur 55

Murkysoft FeeMail 56

Murkysoft NotWork 56

Murkysoft PhoneHome 61

Murkysoft PiggyBank 62

Murkysoft FaxFox 63

The Future of Computing 63

Automatic "Like-it-or-Not" Upgrading 63

Non-Murkysoft Software Cleansing 64

Troubleshooting **67**

Important Murkysoft Phone Numbers 68

Hellllp! 69

Standard Hellllp! 69
Help Topics Criss-Cross Reference Table 70
The Answer Lizard 71
Commonly Asked Questions 71
Existential Concerns 72

Murkysoft Garage 75

Tuner-Upper Kit 75
Murkysoft Minus Kit 76
Fix-a-Flat Kit 76
Front End Alignment Kit 76
Acronymic Miscellaneous Utility
Kit (AMUK) 77

Keyboard Shortcuts 78

Appendices 79
Olfactory Card Smells 81

Glossary of Terms 83

Index 85

Registration Information 91

Foreword by Bill Geeks

Murkysoft Founder
and Chief Dweeb

Hey, dudes. I would like to personally thank you for purchasing WindBlows95.

We at Murkysoft have created an exciting and innovative new interface that takes the best of what our competitors have had for a decade and makes it, well, ours. We think it will soon become the ~~apple~~ peach of your eye. And we think that we soon won't have any competitors (just kidding there, Justice Department folks — heh, heh, last thing we want is to become a nasty old monopoly!).

Some three-initial computer companies think they don't need Murkysoft ... that they can go off and build operating systems (OS) — without *us*! Can you believe it? Well now we're proving that we can make a good OS, too. In fact we thought of naming it OS/Too. Ha ha! Don't be fooled — the three initial computer company reverse-plagiarized WindBlows95 by incorporating virtually all of our features before we even thought of them.

But we're not sensitive about competition. We
think our system is so much better than the ones we,
uh, improved, that comparing them with ours is like
comparing ~~apples~~ bananas and oranges.

I'd like to leave you with a little poem I wrote
(well, actually someone else wrote the original
version of it, and I sort of put my imprimatur on it):

> We've got the look,
> we've got the feel;
> it isn't virtual,
> it's real.
> We own the rights
> to everything,
> you'll use our music
> when you sing.
> You think we're big?
> We'll soon be bigger!
> In fact we'll own,
> the way I figure,
> the Met, the Vatican, and Louvre,
> the U.S. Government and you.
> All hearts and minds will heed our calls,
> because we'll have them by the ... uh, tail.

Notations and Conventions

To make this document especially clear, we will follow the following documentation conventions, as follows:

- We will use periods at the ends of sentences, and commas somewhere in the middle.

- We will not dangle prepositions or anything else you can think of.

- The word online will always be hyphenated.

- We will not be unnecessarily redundant, unless we are required to do so because it is necessary.

- When describing procedures we will use consistent terminology so that while you are performing the task you are not confused by the fact that the process is described as an activity one time and an operation the next.

Special symbols are used throughout this document to convey special meanings. These include:

☞ Hint: Something that will enhance your enjoyment of, or ease your frustration with, WindBlows95.

💣 *Caution: Indicates something potentially hazardous to yourself, your data, or your sanity.*

☠ *Danger: This would be your basic fatal error.*

ॐ Om: You may want to stop here and take a
deep breath and chant Om, to prevent any
homicidal impulses.

꤮ The Blowing Wind: This indicates an area
where we are just blowing wind, talking about
features that don't exist, software that is still
vaporware, or just general hot air. Of course we
don't always warn you when we're doing this.

Lady Justice: If you are an antitrust
lawyer for the government, you should
skip this item — *it's of no interest to you
at all* — really!

Note: Using a new high-technology algorithm
based on recent average SAT verbal scores, this
entire document was completely spell-chucked.

Welcome!

In this section, we will rhetorically ask a number of questions that we would like to answer, and then answer them.

What is WindBlows95?

WindBlows95 is a 32-bit, protected, preemptive multitasking, multithreaded, graphical user interfaced operating system, sort of. But enough bragging. What it means to you, the poor hapless user, is that everything you know and everything you own is now obsolete (see System Requirements).

What is the Messtop Metaphor?

MESS is Murkysoft's Efficient Storage System. We have now made it possible to make your computer as complete a mess as your desktop. We call it a Messtop.

With WindBlows95 you can have more things open than you can possibly work on, so that it is possible to actually lose what you're working on in the confusion of your virtual desktop.

We want to note that old WindBlows had the
concept of multitasking too, but some users felt that
having the *concept* was not enough, that the product
ought to actually allow you to *do* more than one
thing at once without crashing. In WindBlows95
you can do everything at once. If time is nature's
way of making sure everything doesn't happen all
at once, WindBlows95 is our way of making sure it
does.

$ystem Requirements

The advantage of 32-bit architecture is that it is double, that's right, *twice* as much architecture as 16-bit architecture. Which is twice as much as 8-bit, which is twice as much as 4-bit, which is definitely more than 2-bit, unless you have one of the early Pentium chips. Anyway, it's all multiples of 2-bit architecture.

What does this mean to you? It means that everything you now own is obsolete: your computer, your printer, your car, your house, your dog. You will need to purchase the following equipment if you even want to think about running WindBlows95:

- PC with way more memory and disk space than the one you have now (if you don't know the difference between memory and disk space, *don't tell anyone*). Just walk into any store that sells PC hardware and tell them you're upgrading to WindBlows95. They'll be happy to see you!

- Bigger monitor than you have now. Since at any given time there are about 12 toolbars on the screen, if you want to be able to see anything else, you will need a monitor at least as big as your television screen.

- CD-ROM drive, or wait ... maybe something even newer, better ... no, okay, it's still CD-ROM, but please, get *rid* of all those old floppy disks — how embarrassing!

- Sound card, speech recognition card, olfactory card, etc. (see the Multimedia section for the list of *de rigeur* devices); and, to properly control all these cards, of course you'll need a card board.

So with a modest investment of $5,000-$20,000, you can be ready for WindBlows95. Now for WindBlows*96*, that's another story.

Compatibility (i.e. "Crashing")

Your old 16-bit software can run in either protected or shared space. In protected space it will do well, but in shared space 16-bit applications can get on each other's nerves. They may very well corrupt each other. Relationship counseling is suggested.

Badly behaved 32-bit applications can cause WindBlows95 to crash. While this might provide some comforting nostalgia for WindBlows3.1 users, we at Murkysoft do not like for word of this kind of thing to get around. Therefore, any software that causes the system to crash will be sought out and destroyed when you re-boot the computer. If you do not re-boot the computer, Murkysoft Security will be automatically notified via the Murkysoft e-mail system (see section on Bill's World) and you will be sought out and re-programmed.

In the event of a compatibility problem, WindBlows95 will gently make you aware of the problem via a Complete Rapid Accelerated System Halt (CRASH).

Question: Can I run in what used to be called, enigmatically, Real mode?

Answer: Yeah, but it's so, so 1980s, so five-minutes-ago. Get with the program, dude.

Making WindBlows95 Work Like WindBlows3.1

Yes, users with high anxiety can set up WindBlows95 so that it runs exactly the same as WindBlows3.1, including the familiar Program Superintendent. It will perform in all the same ways and do all the same things. In fact, the installation process leaves WindBlows3.1 on your machine and installs only the WindBlows95 startup screen. Impress your friends and your boss with your high-tech-itude, without learning a new interface!

Running WindBlows95 on a 286 or Older Computer

The good news is, yes, you can load WindBlows95 on a 286 or older computer. Once you've done that, tie a long rope to the computer and take it out to your boat. It will make a superb anchor. (You didn't think WindBlows95 would actually *run* on it, did you?)

Features

Here are just a few of the features that will make you glad you have been blown into the WindBlows95 world:

Hyperactive icons

Tired of icons which just sit on your desktop doing absolutely nothing? Now that you have had to invest thousands of dollars in additional memory and computing power, you can put this newfound power to work with WindBlows95 Hyperactive Icons. They're animated. They move around, while remaining in place. Get it? They appear to move around, and around, and around ... while just sitting on your desktop doing absolutely nothing. And, when it gets so bad that you have to scream, your voice recognition card will hear you and ... they will all start to move faster! This alone is worth the price of the software.

Longer File Names

In old WindBlows, file names were limited to 11 characters. This only allowed for a total of about 999,999,999,999 unique file names within a directory (okay, don't check our math on this), certainly not enough to fit in with our MESS concept (described earlier). With WindBlows95 your file names (sometimes known as filenames) can be up to 255 characters (254 wasn't quite enough, 256 would be too much). This now allows for approximately 743 mega-quintupla-bupla-gadzillion unique filenames, and twice as many if you have two computers.

Getting to DOOS

Fortunately, you can still get to good old DOOS (Debilitated Old Operating System). In fact, this is probably the first thing most of you will want to do, just to feel safe. However, we suggest that you Abort, Retry, Ignore, or Fail this habit.

How DOOS Handles Long File Names

If you should be so retro as to try to copy WindBlows95 files with long filenames to a machine running DOOS, not to worry.

If you name a file, say, "My musings on the sad state of the global environment and the dangers to the earth posed by the greenhouse effect," WindBlows95 will automatically read, evaluate and analyze the name, shortening it to an eight-character name that best expresses the nuances of meaning in the longer name. In the above example, WindBlows95 would name the document EAR~001Z.DOC.

By the way, if you counted the characters in that long file name to see that it was less than 255, you may need professional treatment for obsessive-compulsive, anal-retentive behavior. Consult Murkysoft Shrink, your online analyst. (You did count 94, right?)

Sta...sta...stability

WindBlows95 is more stable, and therefore less unstable, than WindBlows3.1. Think of it this way, WindBlows3.1 was like Russian roulette — if you kept playing, eventually you were going to get it. WindBlows95 is more like crossing a busy street — if everybody follows the rules you will probably be okay, unless of course the traffic light goes bippy.

The Short Circuit Bar

This bar is up on the screen all the time, and has stuff on it. So no matter what you're trying to do, there's a little box of stuff floating around in your face.

But don't worry, if you need to move it, you can, and it will even change it's shape and size to better accommodate your viewing needs, for example:

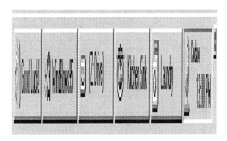

If you feel it's enough to short circuit your wires and make you thrust the mouse through your monitor screen, click on the little X in the upper right-hand corner, and it will go away, at least for a few minutes.

Exhumer

This invaluable tool let's you dig around on your disk to find and exhume files that have been buried deep within layer after layer of folder, or directory, or whatever they are. Just click on the Exhumer icon — if you can find it.

This page unintentionally left blank. Sorry.

Getting Started

In this section we will get started.

Getting Started

In this subsection we will really get started.

Okay, you say, so let's *start me up* (hey, that would make a great song title).

To get started in WindBlows95, do the following:

1) First install the software.

2) Okay, now you're up and running and everything is fine, right? If not, go back and repeat step 1. If you have problems with step 1, see the section on Troubleshooting. If you have problems with the section on Troubleshooting, you may not be compatible with this manual. Anyway, once you're happening you will see the Murkysoft Windblows95 start-up screen:

This is your sign that Murkysoft has taken over your computer. Do not fear, do not attempt to change the channel, and above all, do not attempt to de-install. We are in control. All your old software has been neutralized. You are now entering the "Murkyzone."

3) Okay, now you really are up and running, right? Good. You can already consider yourself special — most people don't get this far.

The WindBlows95 Messtop now appears:

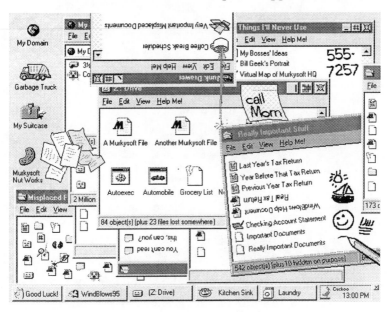

4) Now all you have to do is do something. To start a task, just click on the *GoodLuck* button (in French version this is the *BonVoyage* button, in Spanish, it's the *VayaConDios* button).

This brings up the Windblows95 main task menu:

5) Actually, about the only thing you can do
    directly from this menu is shut down your
    computer. That might not be a bad idea,
    depending on how things went in step 1. Or, if
    you're really ambitious, go ahead to the next
    step.

6) There are two ways to start a task from the *GoodLuck* button. You can select the *Run* option, or you can choose to stay and fight. Ha, ha, just a Murkysoft joke. When you select *Run*, you then simply tell the computer what you want to do. For example if you want to play the game Bungee Jumper, you might tell the computer something like "Yo, I wanna run:

C:\PROGRAMS\GAMES\BUNGEE\BUNGEE.EXE"

but without the Yo part. This is known as "Giving a Command by Typing the Drive, Path, and Executable Program Name." Now you know why we call it *Run*.

7) The second way to start a task is by using the submenus, sub-submenus, sub-sub-submenus, and so on, to find the program you want to run. This is how you would run a non-Murkysoft program (not recommended). To do this, select *Do Other Stuff*. You will get a submenu of other stuff:

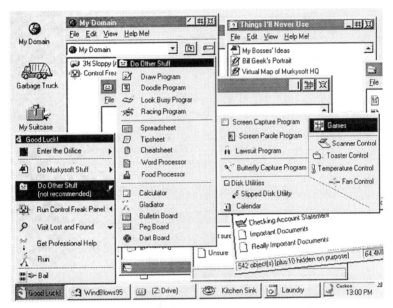

8) When you select something from the submenu,
   a sub-submenu of other stuff will pop-up
   somewhere on your screen. Can you find the
   sub-submenu in the screen below?

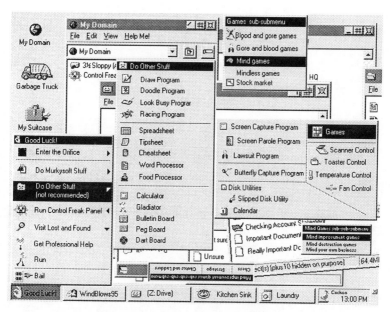

5) Once you have found the sub-submenu of other stuff, you can select something and bring up a sub-sub-submenu of other stuff. Eventually, you will run out of submenus and will have to actually do something. If at any point you run out of submenus and still haven't gotten to a task, try the *Run* option.

6) Well, now you've gotten started. Time to shut down. Or as we say at Murkysoft, *Bail!*

This page intentionally has this sentence on it.

Bailing Out

To end a session, select the same button you would to start a session (really!) — the *GoodLuck* button. Think of it this way: you're starting the ending of the session.

1) From the *GoodLuck* menu, select *Bail!*. You will be prompted to determine your comfort level with various approaches to the concept of egress:

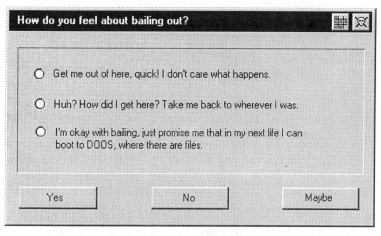

2) Try to get in touch with that part of yourself that feels it needs to escape. Could there be something deeper going on here?

3) If you feel that exiting is not simply your defense against your own fears of abandonment, you may go ahead and bail.

4) Select the Bail option of your choice and click the appropriate button, Yes, No, or Maybe.

Something goes here. Now what was it?

The Basics

In this section, we talk about some of the basics that are basically a basic part of the basic system, in order to give you a basic understanding of what we basically see as ... well, you get the basic idea.

Printing to Toast

The Murkysoft vision of your future is one in which our software controls your entire life. Our current step in this direction is control of your household appliances by treating them as peripheral devices.

Imagine the fun you can have, for example, by printing your documents on a piece of toast! With our special toaster driver and toaster parallel port adapter, your toaster can toast a pattern onto a piece of toast — text, graphics, your imagination is the only limit: print out invitations to a brunch, even send toast-mail messages to your family:

Good Morning, dear. I've left with the kids and I'm never coming back. I've had all I can take. The butter is on the counter.

☞ Hint: English muffins and pumpernickel bread are not recommended as printing media. Also, note that toasters print in black and white or grayscale only.

Hot Tips

Built into lots of Murkysoft software is the concept of tips. We give you little tips that we think you might find helpful or entertaining.

For example, when you start your spreadsheet program we might give you a tip on the current horse races available through OTB, such as:

Tip: "Lucky Lady" in the 8th at Saratoga.

You can take this into consideration as you use the spreadsheet to analyze the OTB data you have downloaded via Murkysoft Bill's World. Of course, Murkysoft accepts no liability for the accuracy of the tip.

Other tips may be more metaphysical in nature, with helpful insights such as:

Tip: A leechee nut in the hand of a fool is like an age without a name.

Likewise, Murkysoft accepts no liability for the accuracy of this information, apparent though it may seem.

Wallpaper

Like the old WindBlows, WindBlows95 lets you select wallpaper for your computer. What's new in WindBlows95 is that, with the proper peripheral devices, you can "wallpaper" your entire house.

Wallpapering a Room

1) To wallpaper a room, select *Run ControlFreak* from the *GoodLuck* menu.

2) From the *ControlFreak Panel*, select something that you think might have the *Wallpaper* feature hiding under it.

3) Select *Wallpaper Room*.

4) Select one of the available designer patterns, shown below:

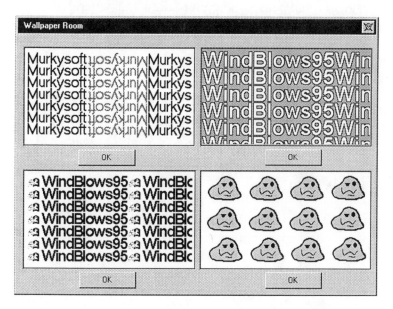

5) Position your printer near the first wall to be "papered" and press Enter. Refer to the printer notes below for correct printer positioning and precautions.

Inkjets

If using an inkjet printer, the printer will spray ink on the wall in the desired color and pattern. Be sure inkjets are pointing towards wall.

💣*Caution: Remove all children and pets from the room before wallpapering with an inkjet printer.*

Plotters

If using a plotter, the plotter will vibrate over to the wall and the pens will begin to draw the pattern. On older model plotters, you may have to manually carry the plotter over to the wall and boost it up to reach the high spots.

Thermal printers

💣*Caution: If using a thermal printer, be sure to remove all flammable objects from the room before wallpapering.*

Hot Wax Printers

☞ Hint: Using a hot wax printer is not recommended in warm climates, since the wallpaper may run on hot days.

Note that the hot wax printer may be used to remove unwanted body hairs, using Murkysoft Body (sold separately).

Task Lizards

Many of the tasks in WindBlows95 and other Murkysoft products have a special help feature known as a **Lizard**. A Lizard is a clever little creature that will help you slither effortlessly through any task, like a Newt through mud (with due apologies to any congressional leaders who may, coincidentally, have lizard-like names).

Getting into waters that are over your head? Stuck in the muck? When you see this symbol:

 It means a Lizard is available to help you.

Click on the Lizard and it will do the task for you. All you have to do is pretty much just stand back and watch. You will get to make a few choices along the way, just to make you feel involved (it's good for your self-esteem).

Navigating In the Carpal Tunnel

The good news is, to get anywhere in WindBlows95 all you have to do is click. And click. And click some more. And keep on clicking on things, opening things, selecting things by clicking on them, until you get where you want to be, or develop Carpal Tunnel Syndrome, whichever comes first.

That's why we call our navigation system the Carpal Tunnel.

Not only can you click, you can drag.

Just be careful when dragging files to keep your mouse on the mouse pad. If you drag the mouse too far you might inadvertently drag your file right off the computer.

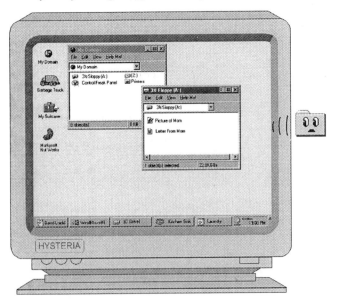

☞ Of course you can always use our navigation
   shortcut method — just go to DOOS, the
   Delapidated Old Operating System, and type
   away!

Murkysoft Orifice

Think of Murkysoft Orifice as the big black hole into which you pour all your information. And money. It does everything. Throw in your silver and we'll polish it; your dry cleaning, and we'll clean it. Count on Murkysoft to totally take you to the cleaners.

Murkysoft Orifice consists of a complete set of productivity tools, which you can use to make people think you are productive. By buying these products and putting the boxes on the shelf, you will appear computer literate. You will find it easier to get dates; small children will no longer make fun of you.

Within the vortex of Murkysoft Orifice, you will find the following fine software packages.

Murkysoft Sentence

While other companies give you word processors, we process entire sentences. If we don't like one of your sentences, we will suggest alternatives with more gooder grammar.

If we do like your sentences, we will send them via Murkysoft e-mail to our database of good sentences which will be made available to other Murkysoft users, which is, basically, everyone. At Murkysoft we believe that good ideas, unless they're ours, are to be shared.

Murkysoft SheetLoad of Numbers

The spreadsheet that, well, spreads things out.
Many people, taking spread and sheet literally,
think that our spreadsheet can make your bed. This,
obviously, is beyond the capabilities of any PC
software. It can, however, iron pillowcases if you
have the proper parallel port adapter for your iron.

Murkysoft Excess

The database that gives you more than you need. In
fact if you don't have any data, our **Data Lizard**
will create some for you — for example, a random
mailing list with some very impressive addresses
and graphics so you can print out labels suitable for
framing. Want to have the income tax returns of
your friends, your employer, your congressman?
Use our Data Lizard to get any data you want.

Other Bundled Stuff

Practically Error-Free Calculator

New improved version! It makes no math errors!
At least not so far.

Scheduler, with Dynamic Slippage Feature

Creates your own personal schedule. Comes pre-filled with Murkysoft product announcement dates, release dates, and upgrade dates. This way you can anticipate our products when they're announced, buy them as soon as they're released, and actually *use* them once the first upgrade comes out. And the dates automatically slip to keep in synch with our own slipping delivery dates. (Look for WindBlows96 sometime in '98!)

Installing New Hardware

Installing new hardware on a PC used to be a frustrating process, fraught with difficulty.

Now, in WindBlows95, we have a **Hardware Lizard** that slithers you through the process of installing new hardware. No longer do you need to know the proper DMA channels (however you do need to know your personal DNA code). No longer must you assign irksome IRQ interrupts to the new hardware, only to find out that you have disabled the old hardware — WindBlows95 will automatically assign the IRQ interrupts and disable your old hardware for you.

Plug and Play

Plug and Play is the magical process by which you just stick the card that runs a new piece of hardware in the computer and, vôilà, it actually works! Remember, however, for Plug and Play to work, the following must be true:

- Computer must be Plug and Play

- Card must be Plug and Play

- Day must be Tuesday

- Year must be leap

If any of the above are not true, you may find that you can Plug but not Play, or Play but not Plug (this is known as foreplay).

If you have a problem with installing new hardware, maybe you are hot docking when you should be warm docking, cool docking, or shock jocking. If you are not familiar with these exciting new buzzwords, call your hardware manufacturer (do NOT call Murkysoft under any circumstances — we're not going to be available).

If you have difficulties with Plug and Play, we suggest you try:

Pub and Pay

If Plug and Play makes you shrug and pray, try Pub and Pay. Pub and Pay is an innovative new approach to computing wherein you go to the **pub** and have a beer while **pay**ing someone else to get the computer working. (If you are in a 12-step program you may substitute appropriately for the pub part.)

Using Networks

We support NetBEUI, IPX/SPX, TCP/IP, and AFL/CIO network protocols.

If you have trouble installing or using your network with WindBlows95, call your hardware vendor. If they don't support WindBlows95, you've got a real problem, and we'd like to help you. Unfortunately, we're really busy working on other important problems like world domination, suing people, being sued, etc., so you can imagine just how concerned we are that you, whoever you are, are having a bad network day.

ॐ If you are having network problems, it's important to remember to breath deeply. You may want to try some inverted yoga postures to increase blood flow to your brain.

Post no bills.

Multimedia

Welcome to the exciting new world of multimedia, in which media multiply and follow you around wherever you go. WindBlows95 supports multimedia for all the senses: sight, sound, smell, touch, taste, and sixth. Below are examples of some of the media we support.

Olfactory card

At last, your computer can generate smells. Isn't this what your life has been missing? A bad smell is an error message; the smell of warm bread means your document is ready at the toaster (see Printing to Toast).

Thermal card

Heats up your CD-ROM drive to 475 degrees for toasting bagels (slice thin); lower setting can be used to make dried fruit (slice thin); Caution: if turned up too high can create vaporware.

"Ultra" Sound Card

 Ever hear of the rock band who achieves extra volume by using amps that go to 11 instead of the usual 10? The WindBlows95 Ultra Sound Card driver lets you set volume levels from 1-11 instead of from a mere 1-10. You've got to admit, 11 is more.

Other Special Drivers

WindBlows95 supplies a variety of special drivers
that teach your old devices new tricks.

Virtual Device Drivers

You may have heard of virtual device drivers,
which are for virtual devices. A virtual device is a
device that is virtually there, or might be there but
really isn't, and when you consider that in any
given molecule there is more space than matter, is
anything really here? So don't worry about virtual
devices. It's actual devices that you should be
worried about.

Plotter Tattoo Driver

This driver, part of Murkysoft Body, turns your
plotter into an automatic tattoo machine. Just create
the design in your favorite drawing program, lay
your arm on the plotter, and let 'er rip. We have
even provided some tattoo designs you can use:

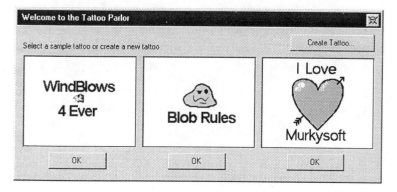

Aerodynamic Fan Driver

This driver turns the common window fan into a musical flying vehicle. The fan will fly around the room, humming a simple mindless tune. Children will love it! Use an extension cord to extend the flight path.

💣 *Not recommended for ceiling fans, as they may cause the entire house to move, and you may find that you're not in Kansas any more.*

Controlling the Weather

📫 As part of our effort to control as much of your environment as possible, WindBlows95 introduces a revolutionary new concept, weather control. This is a powerful new feature that you undoubtedly will find very exciting.

Since it is a revolutionary new feature, it is not yet as robust as our revolutionary old features, or our evolutionary new features. In other words, it does not in fact work at all in this version.

The beta version is good at producing thunderstorms, but unfortunately the storms cause a power outage, preventing the software from continuing to operate.

If you are interested in this feature, be sure to buy WindBlows96, which will come out in 1998.

Bill's World

Think of Bill Geeks and Murkysoft as the spider in
the center of the WorldWide Web. Bill's World is
the giant umbrella that will leave you high and dry
in the world of connectivity and mixed metaphors.

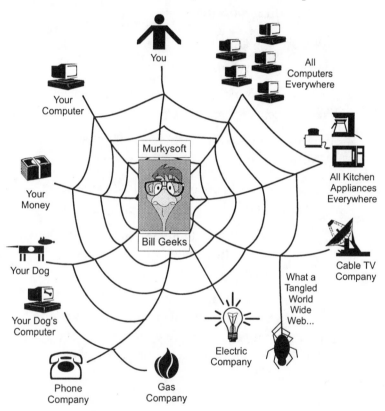

Bill's World is the master program that manages the messages from our suite of message-making software:

- Murkysoft FeeMail

- Murkysoft NotWork

- Murkysoft PhoneHome

- Murkysoft PiggyBank

- Murkysoft FaxFox

Bill's World also includes access to "third party" online services:

- Internet (soon to be MurkyNet) via Internet Voyeur

- CompuSurf and America All Mine (soon to be subsidiaries of Murkysoft)

- Other MAPI-capable mail systems (for you non-technical types, this stands for May Appear Partially Intact)

In the future we will support a new Murkysoft protocol *MS*ATT, after our acquisition of a certain telecommunications company which we cannot disclose at this time. (Note: the name may be changed to *MS*MCI.)

If you are a Justice Department anti-trust investigator, please skip the next sentence (it's just a joke, anyway, ha ha). We will see to it that this becomes the worldwide standard. All future software will support it (since all future software will be made by us.)

Internet Voyeur

To access the Internet, you can use our viewer, the Internet Voyeur (IV). IV plugs you into all the interesting material out there on the Information Superhighway. Voyeur lets you peek into other people's computers, poke around in their closets and desk drawers, if you will. If you are an information junkie, you'll want to use IV!

Note: While the Internet itself is not yet a division of Murkysoft, negotiations are underway aimed at privatizing the system, now wastefully run at public expense. Chairman Bill anticipates an announcement of the new system — MurkyNet — around Christmas, 1996. The MurkyNet will dispense with the dizzying array of "access providers" now confusing the consumer and replace them with a simplified and centralized "gateway" to all the world's data.

Murkysoft FeeMail

FeeMail is the politically correct[1] e-mail system that makes it easy to send messages to anyone in the known universe. It's almost as good as the post office, but of course not quite as reliable. Don't be misled by the name — it works for all genders.

It's simple: you send mail, you pay fee. You get mail, you pay fee. You don't do anything for a month, you pay fee. The way we see it at Murkysoft, the best things in life are fees.

Murkysoft NotWork

This is one online network that will truly live up to its name. Other online services make great claims. We guarantee that Murkysoft NotWork will provide you with so many hours of online time that are totally wasted and non-productive that you will Not get any Work done whatsoever.

---

[1] After extensive market research that seems to indicate that roughly half of the entire population consists of humans of the female persuasion, Murkysoft has named its "mail" system to be, if not gender neutral, at least affirmatively non-patriarchal. If you have no idea what we are talking about here, then you probably have no idea what we are talking about.

Here are the answers to some commonly asked questions, asked by common people like yourself.

What is Murkysoft NotWork?

> Murkysoft NotWork is the biggest, the baddest, the most complete online service on the planet, except of course for some of the others. The NotWork is the product of some 50,000 Murkysoft employees working some 500,000,000 person hours, without sleeping or eating. In a tribute to that dedication, the bones of five Murkysoft technicians who collapsed from exhaustion while trying to make deadline on the project were ground up and used to create a dignified plaque, a virtual image of which you can access via Murkysoft NotWork (access the mail address: dust@murkysoft.com).

What's available on the Murkysoft NotWork?

> Our designers have anticipated the 'Net surfer's every need, from front-row tickets at the all-star MurkyStock online concert to upfront and personal "chat" sessions with Bill Geeks himself ($100/minute). Head spinning from the huge variety on the old-fashioned Internet? Murkysoft NotWork cuts the clutter and brings you only the information that we want you to ... er, that is, that you will want to know.

Will I still be able to use my old services, like CompuServe, America On Line and Prodigy?

That would be nice wouldn't it, if we didn't have to have change in our lives? But the world isn't like that, is it?

No, you see, because of the special 32-bit operating system at the heart of WindBlows95 and new more efficient protocols (XQMZ/99, IPQ/XXUE, FUBAR/U2) use of these technically outdated forums is not encouraged.

In fact, the WindBlows95 installation program anticipates this very problem by automatically removing all traces of these services from your computer's hard drive. In addition, proprietary "Web browsers" like LimberMosaic and NewtCruiser will be safely disabled.

While it is possible to reconnect to these antiquated services (please contact Murkysoft Psychiatric Services at insane@murkysoft.com before proceeding), the procedure is complicated and requires installation of the $395 Garbage Hauler program. Installing the Murkysoft NotWork, however, is a simple operation that you perform right from the Messtop.

Do I have to connect to Murkysoft NotWork to run WindBlows95?

No, but because it's expected that most WindBlows95 customers (we prefer to call them "friends") will want Murkysoft NotWork, the program automatically assigns you a "user name" (based on what our Research Department says was your "handle" in high school) and deducts the $200 "initiation fee" from your bank account (see On-Line Banking). Your Murkysoft NotWork account can, of course, be canceled, by simply blurfing your smoogle-wonk.

Is registration a painful procedure, like a root canal?

No, you must be thinking of hardware installation. When you first sign on to Murkysoft NotWork, you'll be prompted for your address, telephone number, credit card numbers, home alarm security code, SAT scores, income level, and marital indiscretion history. Once we've got all that, you're in! And don't worry about "double billing" - Murkysoft will automatically cancel your accounts at the other on-line services

What kind of member assistance is available?

Murkysoft NotWork's on-line representatives are standing by to assist you in accessing and understanding current billing information. You can even access your current account status on-line! Should making the monthly payments slip your mind, we will...well, we'll let billing assistants Slats and Bruno tell you about that — off-line!

Can I, like, get into the cool porno groups on Usenet and the Web?

You slime. Don't even think about accessing any pornography on-line, unless of course you're talking about Michelangelo's David or various other *au naturel* works of digital art that are now owned exclusively by Murkysoft.

The Murkysoft NotWork is equipped with BAREness Alert Sensing Software (we just couldn't think of an acronym for it!) which, upon detecting unauthorized carnal exposure, will: a) automatically disable your computer; b) cause a loud, piercing alarm to issue from your stereo speakers; c) compose and mail a stern letter to your parents, teachers, or spousal equivalent.

Murkysoft PhoneHome

 WindBlows95 supports a telephone interface. However, since most phones don't have faces, this doesn't help you much. Also, technically there is no software, at least on this planet, now, that works with it.

However, in the future, you will be able to call and talk to your computer, much like you would to a friend or spouse — the computer will even hang up on you if you raise your voice.

For example, you could call from the upstairs phone in the morning to instruct the computer to make toast, so that it will be ready when you come downstairs. Of course you would have to put the bread in the toaster the night before, or come down and put bread in the toaster then go back upstairs and call. See how much easier your life will be in the Murkysoft future?

Murkysoft PiggyBank

 Yes, it is possible to do your banking from the comfort of your own home using the global reach of the Murkysoft on-line network. Just click on the fistful-of-greenbacks icon that's part of the Bill's World screen. Without leaving your keyboard, you'll be able to open or close an account, deposit or withdraw money, and obtain loan and credit information. Because we already took this vital information from you as part of the network sign-on process, Murkysoft can, for your convenience, automatically deduct our monthly payments from your checking or savings accounts.

It has been brought to our attention by some students in Berkeley, California that, because of a minor "glitch" in the basic security structure of the Internet, anyone with even primitive "hacking" skills will also be able to access your credit history and banking accounts, withdraw your money, or take out large unsecured loans in your name.

(This type of flaw, which points to the basic inefficiencies of government-led services, is guaranteed not to occur after the Murkysoft Internet "privatization," scheduled for Christmas, 1996.)

To safeguard your financial security while the "glitch" is being remedied, Murkysoft NotWork is requiring each user to personally pledge, on-line, that they will not tamper with other members' records. We believe that this "honor" system will be an effective protection.

Murkysoft FaxFox

With this wonderful product you can blah, blah, blah, send faxes, blah, blah, blah, high tech ... global village ... all that, blah, blah, blah. You need it.

The Future of Computing

Thanks to the power (ours, that is) inherent in a world of interconnected computers, Murkysoft has developed a vision of the future. The good news is, you're in it. The bad news is ... oh, come on now, you didn't really think there would be any *bad* news, did you? Just leave it to Murkysoft, we'll take care of everything!

Automatic "Like-it-or-Not" Upgrading

The future of computing is: WindBlows96, WindBlows97, WindBlows98 ... and we want to make sure you are on board for the future.

Therefore, your version of WindBlows95 will become obsolete at midnight on December 31st, 1995 (according to your local time zone), and will self-destruct at that time.

Don't worry, your data is safe, and you will be able to access it ... as soon as WindBlows96 is installed. The really great news is that we will automatically download WindBlows96 to you during the last week of December. At the same time we will automatically install it and bill your credit card in time to have you up and running when the big ball drops in Times Square. *Happy New Year from Murkysoft!*

☞ Note: In the *highly unlikely* event of software release delays, we will go to Plan B. Refer to the *Murkysoft Windblows95 Technical Reference* for details. This book will be available in March of 1996, good lord willin' and the creek don't rise.

Non-Murkysoft Software Cleansing

When you install any Murkysoft product, we automatically detect any software on your system not made by Murkysoft and delete it — of course, we replace it with our own version and if we don't have a version we just attach our logo to the existing product, send out new product announcements, and send you a bill. Also see our Minus Kit for performing this process manually.

Of course you won't really be able to use the product until we complete our alpha test and beta test, and our chi test, and our delta test, and our epsilon test, and so on, till we finally do a zeta test. Then we know that the product is ready to be released because we've run out of Greek letters.

This page intentionally left blank.

Geeks is a megalomaniac.

Unless you're one to read between the lines.

Troubleshooting

No matter what happens, do NOT call Murkysoft.
We are not open now. If the error occurs while you
are using hardware, please contact your hardware
vendor. And remember, the answers, my friend, are
blowing in the wind.

Problem	Solution
Document printed on toast is too dark.	Check toaster setting. Toast may be burned. Do not attempt to print on pumpernickel.
Document printing in toaster explodes.	You have probably attempted to print to a PopTart. Please select a printing media from the Toaster Printing Media guide in the Appendix.
After 15 minutes of operation my '84 Volvo emits a slight burning smell.	The blower motor is probably burning out. Use the Murkysoft ControlFreak Panel to run a test.
After 15 minutes of using Windblows95 my computer emits a slight burning smell.	The blower motor is probably burning out. Using oven mitts, quickly throw computer out the window before it explodes.
When I try to access Help for a topic, I get answers that have nothing to do with the topic I requested.	You have a problem with that? Picky, picky. See the Help Topics Criss-Cross Reference Table in the *Hellllp!* section.
When I boot I get the message "Welcome to WindBlows95."	You have justifiable cause for alarm. However, this is normal. Take a deep breath and proceed.

Important Murkysoft Phone Numbers

Dept.	Phone #	Hours
SALES	**1-800-BUY-MORE**	**OPEN 24 HOURS**
Tech Support	1-900-PLS-HOLD	In your time zone, the hours are 3 a.m. – 4 a.m., on alternate odd Tuesdays.

Hellllp!

We knew you'd be turning to this section.
Screaming for help? We have a very
comprehensive, if not comprehensible, help system
in WindBlows95. It has two fantastic, if not
functional, parts:

- Standard *Hellllp!*
- Answer Lizard

Standard Hellllp!

Normally Standard *Hellllp!* doesn't need much
explanation — if you need help on your help system
you know you're in trouble, eh? Well, in the
current release of WindBlows95 there is a slight
problem — actually we couldn't call it a bug
because our Quality Assurance department would
not release software with a bug in it, so we refer to
it as an Intentional Design Error, or IDE.

Anyway, this IDE results in the wrong help
information coming up when you select a topic.
Well, it's not so much that the information is
wrong. The information is correct, it just doesn't
pertain to the topic you selected. So ... here is a
handy table to help you find the *Hellllp!*
information that *does* pertain to the topic you need.

Help Topics Criss-Cross Reference Table

If you want *Helllp!* on:	Ask for *Helllp!* on:
Add programs	Printing multiple copies
Address book	Add programs
America On Line	(No Help Available)
Arrange icons	Disk management software *or* Zmodem protocol (this is an example of multi-threading)
Auto Hide	Auto Seek
Autoexec.bat	Herakles Strangling the Nemean Lion
Anything other than the above	A full *Hellllp!* conversion key is available, but you didn't think we were going to give it away, did you? Send $10.95 to Bill's Buy the Louvre Campaign, 1 Murkysoft Place, Murkysoft, Washington.

The Answer Lizard

 The Answer Lizard lets you ask any question you want and WindBlows95 will answer it if, of course, you ask one of the questions we have programmed answers to, and let's add another phrase here to avoid a dangling preposition.

You can look these answers up at any time, but we have reprinted a few of the more frequently asked answers here, for your convenience.

Commonly Asked Questions

Question: Where have all my directories and files gone?

> They have been sent by Murkysoft FeeMail to our world headquarters where they are being spell checked, edited, renamed, encrypted, and plagiarized. They will then be sent to the Internet where they can be easily accessed under the address:
>
> ```
> HTTP\\XYZ\\@WindBlows95.Murkysoft.com.
> files.[yournamehere].1500pennsylvania.
> ave//!@#$%^&*()_+|\\[enter PIN
> number].okay.that's.enough.over?
> ```
>
> Any questionable content will be sent to Jesse Helms for review, which could result in user being clicked and dragged out of the country.

Question: Why do I need to learn a totally new interface?

Because the totally old interface is so, well, so five-minutes-ago. Besides, this interface isn't so new, our competitors have used it for years.

Question: How do I get out of here?

You can't. Once you install WindBlows95, you no longer have control of your machine. But if you're feeling that panicky feeling, just keep clicking on anything that looks like an X and it will get rid of most of the stuff on your screen ... for now.

Will my old applications run?

Only if they have legs. Ha ha! No, seriously, WindBlows95 is backwardly compatible with previous versions of WindBlows, so your old applications will run, but backwards. We are forwardly compatible with all the new software you will have to buy in the future that we haven't even thought of yet.

Existential Concerns

Is God dead?

No, Murkysoft is doing fine, thanks.

If I'm not in real mode, am I real?

No. You're not real even if you are in real mode. You are just a figment of your computer's imagination.

Where does the light from my computer screen go, ultimately?

Since light is energy, is may be transformed into matter, in which case, since it's mind over matter, matter must be under mind, which undermines our undertaking to understand this but sheds no light on the possible effects on the price of pork futures.

DEAR
   EDITOR -
LET'S MAKE SURE
WE DON'T LEAVE
THIS PAGE
   BLANK!

Murkysoft Garage

Murkysoft Garage is a set of utilities that will make WindBlows95 run like a race car. Imagine this, the wind is blowing in your face at 140 mph as you round that hairpin turn and, oh no! An oil slick! And it's 16-bit! You feel your wheel spin as the car loses control and … Now don't you wish you had bought Murkysoft Garage?

With Murkysoft Garage, WindBlows95 will run like, well, like the way you would want it to run anyway. But if we included it with WindBlows95 many of our loyal users would be deprived of the chance to buy more Murkysoft Software.

Murkysoft Garage includes:

Tuner-Upper Kit

Includes everything to fine tune your software engine. We don't include replacement hoses, since we gave you ample hosing in the original WindBlows95 version.

Murkysoft Minus Kit

Searches your disk for any non-Murkysoft Software and deletes it. You will have a chance to confirm whether or not you want to delete the software. However, we will delete it anyway, regardless of your answer.

Fix-a-Flat Kit

This includes a compressor, which compresses your disk. Well, it really compresses what's on your disk so it takes up less space (we're talking electronic space here, virtual space, sort of like theoretical, cyberspace). However, compression takes time, like hours, maybe days. It's the old space-time continuum. When you compress, you have more space, but less time.

Front End Alignment Kit

Does everything you do seem to go off track? Do you list to port when you're steering to starboard? Well the Front End Alignment Kit certainly can't help with that. It will, however, line up all your icons one behind the other so that your desktop will always appear neat, even when you've got more open files than the CIA.

Acronymic Miscellaneous Utility Kit (AMUK)

Okay, we know amok is spelled with an "o", we *know* that. Nonetheless, the AMUK utilities will let you run amok to your heart's content. It includes the following programs:

FBI - Front Back Inside

Randomly rearranges your data ... or someone else's.

CIA - Completely Inaccessible Access

Assigns password protection to other people's software, so you can access it, but they can't!

IRS - Inscrutable Reporting System

Reports all your financial data in a form so complicated that the IRS will do anything to avoid having to audit you.

Keyboard Shortcuts

Any WindBlows95 task can be performed by
pointing, clicking, dragging, clicking, pointing, etc.,
with the mouse. However, if you have one of those
old-fashioned computers that still has a keyboard,
you can use some of these handy shortcuts to
accomplish common tasks.

Task	Keyboard Shortcut
Quick exit	Ctrl+Alt+Del
Switching to another application	Alt-Tab-Pepsi-Coke
Saving a file	Ctrl+Shift+Alt+Esc+Spacebar +CapsLock+PgUp
Blowing away a file	Ctrl+Shift+Alt+Esc+Spacebar +CapsLock+PgDn
Adding boldface to text while simultaneously printing to toast, collating the loaf of bread, and closing everything that's open	Alt+Esc+F3+B+Q+F3+$\sqrt{43}$
Accessing Help	F13

Appendices

What, you think we're gonna put something funny
on every otherwise blank page?

Olfactory Card Smells

As a service to our multimedia users we have reprinted here some highly useful information about smells that can be generated by your olfactory card.

This is from "The Effects of Odors on Penile Blood Flow," a study conducted by Dr. Alan Hirsch, the neurological director of the Smell & Taste Treatment and Research Foundation in Chicago. Hirsch gave male volunteers masks scented with a variety of odors and odor combinations, and then recorded the men's level of sexual arousal, as measured by penile blood flow. Reprinted with permission from *Harper's Magazine*, September 1995 issue. Really.

Murkysoft accepts no responsibility for what readers may decide to do with this information.

Scent	Increase in penile blood flow (avg.)
Lavender and pumpkin pie	40%
Doughnut and black licorice	32%
Pumpkin pie and doughnut	20%
Orange	20%
Black licorice	13%
Doughnut and cola	13%
Buttered popcorn	9%
Musk	8%
Cola	7%
Cheese pizza	5%
Roasting meat	5%
Cinnamon buns	4%
Baby powder	3%
Chocolate	3%

Hey, we're not making this up!

Glossary of Terms

Disk-cashing: This refers to putting more money into your hard disk. Of course, cashing is not strictly necessary, you can use disk-credit instead.

Multithreaded: A communication system that lets you follow a thread of thought or conversation and take it wherever it leads you, sort of like free association, free, born free, free to run like the wind blows, free like WindBlows, free? fee! free-fee-whee-me-gee, see?

Preemptive multitasking: Multitasking that will preempt the David Letterman show if you have something really cool to show to a television audience.

Protected: Not unprotected. WindBlows95 is a 32-bit protected environment, and these days it's a good idea to protect your bits.

Synchronous SRAM: As the name suggests, this is SRAM that is synchronized to the clock speed of your computer. Thus, on a 133-MHz computer, if your clock is ten minutes slow, your SRAM will be too. Unfortunately, no one knows what SRAM is.

Index

America On Line
  replacing with Murkysoft NotWork, 19
Apple Corporation
  see Plagiarism, reverse
Bill's World
  connecting everything to everything, 14
  emergency help when it all disconnects, 14
CD Player
  using to load WindBlows95, 1
  using to experience other fine Murkysoft
       products, 2
CompuServe
  replacing with Murkysoft NotWork, 93
Connecting
  to a printer, 87
  to a toaster, 88
  to a spiritual advisor, 89
CONFIG.SYS file
  scary stories about idiots who fiddled with, 310
Copying WindBlows95 discs
  jail sentences for, 55
  viruses triggered by, 56
Defragmenting
  your disk, 57
  your mind after installation, 58
Devices, Peripheral
  see Peripheral Devices
DOOS
  how to get to, (see Relief)
  ordering version 7.0, 46

Drag and Drop
    files, 160
    bodies, 161
Exchange
    reading e-mail in, 188
    reading faxes in, 189
    Murkysoft surveillance of, 190
Exiting to DOOS
    getting Bill's permission, 191
Extensions
    on files, 155
    on loans to buy more hardware, 156
File Names, Long
    descriptive, even prosaic possibilities using, 2
    inability of your "other" word processor to read, 9
Files
    finding, 00
    losing, 45-46
    (see also: Undelete, Moments of silent prayer)
Folders
    as bold new concept, no longer directories, 140
    as same thing as directories, 140
    containing other folders, 141
Freezing Up
    see: Installing New Hardware
Geeks, Bill
    sending e-mail to, 25
    personal guarantee from, 2-3
    tithing protocols for, 6
Help Menu
    getting help with, 14
    fixing bugs of, 18
    translations into English, 15

Hyperactive Icons
    getting them to stop, 8
Internet
    planned purchase of by Murkysoft, 180
Loading
    from CD-ROM discs, 110
    from floppy discs, 111
    from bootleg discs bought in Hong Kong, 112
Minus Kit
    using to remove competitor's software, 81
Modems
    external, 250
    internal, 250
    infernal, 251-290
Mouse
    droppings, 201
MurkySerfs
    (see Employment Opportunities)
Murkysoft NotWork
    art masters on, 69
    billing from, 70
    connecting to, 71
    superiority of, 72
Multitasking
    opening 27 programs at once, 6
    doing nothing while appearing to be, 6
    on 386 computer, see: Meltdowns
Murkysoft
    attorneys retained by, 65
    legal rights of, 66
Murkysoft SheetLoad of Numbers
    as spreadsheet, 11
    as spreadblanket, 11

Murkysoft Excess
  using to take up gigs of memory, 12
  using to get a gig for your band, 12
Murkysoft FeeMail
  ordering Murkysoft "stamps," 170
  sending "bill-mail," 11
Murkysoft Orifice
  as black hole, 11
Murkysoft Sentence
  superiority to "word" processor, 11
My Computer
  inability to locate drives of, 83
Networks
  ABC, 210
  CBS, 212
  NBC, 211
  MSN, 213
Nineteenth Century Impressionists, 27
On-line Help
  being put on hold by, 67
Passwords
  access to, 200
  (see also, Murkysoft's Rights)
Peripheral Devices
  see Devices, Peripheral
Phone Home
  as bye-bye to Bells, 15
Prodigy
  replacing with Murkysoft NotWork, 296-299
Program Superintendent
  panic over absence of, 121
  retrieving as security blanket, 122

Recycling Bin
   emptying, 99-102
   realizing that important files are lost forever, 103
Safe Recovery
   assurance that it doesn't really exist, 77
Screen Savers
   addictions to, 76
   toaster traumas, 76
Sorcerers
   what to do when the "magic" fails, 119
System Requirements
   hard drive, 7
   RAM, 7
   sound card, 7
   CD-ROM
   (see also, Buying a New Computer)
Start Button
   using to shut down system, 10
Task Bar
   using to check time wasted in Setup fiddling, 130
Tiling
   windows, 71
   Bill Geeks' pool, 72
Wallpaper
   free samples of, 10
   billing plans for, 10
   file-corrupting properties of, 10
WindBlows96
   advance ordering of, 23-25
   global celebration of, 26

•

Registration Information

In order to register your purchase of WindBlows95 with Murkysoft, please complete the form below, cut it out, tape it to your computer screen and select Online Registration to e-mail it to Murkysoft. If that doesn't work, mail to:

> Murkysoft Intelligence Division
> 1 Murkysoft Place
> Murkysoft, Washington

This information will help Murkysoft to send you the right junk mail in the future, and will provide us with valuable information that we can sell to other people who want to send you junk mail.

Name: _____

Address:_____

Home phone number: _____

Fax number: _____

Credit Card Number: _____

ATM Access Codes: _____

Sex:

     ___male ___female ___other

Sexual Preference:

     ___male ___female ___online

Household Income:

     ___ Over $100,000

     ___ $50,000 to $99,000

     ___ Don't bother.

WindBlows95 Serial Number (and we'd better not find out it's registered to someone else!) _____

(We recommend you tattoo this number onto the back of your hand for easy access, and so the software police can identify you if necessary.)

WindBlows95 was purchased from:
___ department store
___ computer store
___ liquor store
___ friend/bootlegger.
If you selected "friend/bootlegger," please supply name and address here: _____

When you asked to purchase WindBlows95, the vendor:
___ laughed
___ cried
___ made a *ch-ching ch-ching* noise and headed for the cash register
___ all of the above.

In the last year, have you purchased:
___ other Murkysoft products
___ subversive literature
___ unauthorized biographies of Bill Geeks
___ any products from software companies named for fruit?

Do you believe in the free-enterprise system?
___ yes ___ no ___ huh?

Really, truly, no matter what?
___ yes ___ yes.

Do you have any major philosophical difficulties with a single company, say Murkysoft, controlling a single global computer operating system, the entire software industry, vast stores of personal demographic data, and the digital imagery of the world's great art treasures?
___no   ___ yes.

No! Don't really send this in! It's a joke!
(you *were* going to send it in, weren't you?)

If you must send something in, see the order form in the back of the book!

It is now safe to shut down your computer.

(Just don't turn it back on.)

Have You Enjoyed this Useless Guide to WindBlows95?

Tell us! Talk to us! Order more copies for your friends and family! We'd love to know who you are and to hear your feedback. You can contact us at:

Hysteria Publications
P.O. Box 8581
Bridgeport, CT 06605
(203) 333-9399
fax (203) 367-7188

or write to us at the following e-mail address (don't use this for ordering):

70410.145@compuserve.com

And ... to find out about other fine humor products from Hysteria Publications, be sure to check out our Internet WorldWide Web Home Page at:

http://www.coolbooks.com/~outpost/pubs/hyst

Also, don't miss the ads on the following pages!

Hey, this was supposed to be page 96, what's going on here?

What is this? This Windblows95 word processor
doesn't seem to be able to paginate beyond page 95!

Due to circumstances beyond our control, all the remaining pages are going to be numbered 95. Other than that, everything will be perfectly normal. perfectly normal. perfectly normal.

IS MARTHA STUART LIVING?
1996 PARODY CALENDAR

Follow the
"dominatrix of domesticity"
through a year of
impossible projects. Shouldn't you
be living in Marthatime?

FULL COLOR WALL CALENDAR 12"x24" OPEN
$12.95

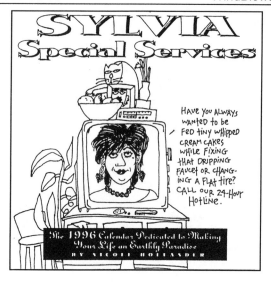

SYLVIA SPECIAL SERVICES
THE 1996 CALENDAR DEDICATED TO
MAKING YOUR LIFE AN EARTHLY PARADISE
BY NICOLE HOLLANDER

How unnecessary your therapist
would be if you had someone
to call your mother every Sunday,
and twice on Mother's Day.
Join others like yourself and let
Sylvia make your life
a constant delight!

COLOR CARTOON CALENDAR 12"X24" OPEN
$12.95

GETTING IN TOUCH
WITH YOUR INNER BITCH
BY ELIZABETH HILTS

For the woman who
wants to laugh out loud
and speak her mind!
The Inner Bitch calls it as she
sees it. This is the end of
Toxic Niceness as we know it.

PAPERBACK
$7.95

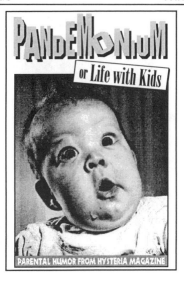

PANDEMONIUM
OR LIFE WITH KIDS

A collection of parental humor
including:
"I Killed June Cleaver",
"Spit-Shining the Kids" and
"Why It Takes Mom a Week to Get
Over the 24-Hour Flu"

PAPERBACK
$7.95

'CAUSE I'M THE MOMMY
(THAT'S WHY)!
BY DONNA BLACK

A unique perspective on
the exhaustion and
exhilaration of motherhood.
Refreshingly honest and funny.
Must reading for every parent!

PAPERBACK
$7.95

Order Form

WindBlows95 — A Useless Guide

Parody User Guide

_____ copies @ $7.95 $_____

Is Martha Stuart Living?

1996 Parody Wall Calendar

_____ copies @ $12.95 $_____

Sylvia Special Services

1996 Cartoon Wall Calendar by Nicole Hollander

_____ copies @ $12.95 $_____

Getting In Touch With Your Inner Bitch

Paperback by Elizabeth Hilts

_____ copies @ $7.95 $_____

Pandemonium (Or, Life With Kids)

Paperback collection of parental humor

_____ copies @ $7.95 $_____

'Cause I'm The Mommy (That's Why)!

Paperback by Donna Black

_____ copies @ $7.95 $_____

At Your Fingertips: The Care & Maintenance of a Vagina

Paperback Hysteria humor collection

_____ copies @ $7.95 $_____

Subtotal $_____

CT Residents add 6% sales tax $_____

Add $3.00 shipping per address
(over $25.00, add $4.00 per addr.) $_____

Total Enclosed $_____

Check or money order only w/ your name, address, & phone to:

Hysteria   Your Name: _____
PO Box 8581   Address: _____
Bridgeport, CT 06605   _____
(203) 333-9399   Phone: _____